And Something Weird Happened...

By Pamela Rushby
Illustrated by Omar Aranda

Pearson Australia
(a division of Pearson Australia Group Pty Ltd)
707 Collins Street, Melbourne, Victoria 3008
PO Box 23360, Melbourne, Victoria 8012
www.pearson.com.au

First published 2010 by Pearson Australia
2018 2017 2016 2015
10 9 8 7 6 5 4 3 2

Publisher: Simone Calderwood
Illustrator: Omar Aranda/The Illustrators Agency
Editors: Lisa Warden and Sophie Ayerbe
Designer: Glen McClay
Copyright & Pictures Editor: Helen Mammides
Project Editor: Aisling Coughlan
Production Controller: Claire Henry
Printed in Australia by the SOS Print + Media Group

ISBN 978 1 4425 2815 4

Pearson Australia Group Pty Ltd ABN 40 004 245 943

Contents

Chapter 1

A Very Boring Holiday

IT WAS OUR FIRST WEEK back at school after the holidays. And our new teacher wanted us to write about what we'd done over the holidays.

"You must have done some exciting things!" she said. "What did you do, Rosie?"

"We went to the beach," said Rosie. "We stayed in a caravan and surfed every day."

"Lovely!" said our new teacher. "Someone else?"

Everyone had done something good. Tom's cousin had come to stay. Tom's cousin was a skateboard champ. He'd taught Tom some really good tricks.

Yuki had been on a plane to visit her grandparents in Japan.

Ben had been to a basketball camp. Everyone had done something good. Except me.

I'd had the most boring holiday on the planet. My mum had to work, so I'd stayed home, day after day, with my little sister, Natalie. My gran came to look after us.

We'd done really exciting stuff—played on the swings at the park, listened to story time at the library and swum in the local pool. We had watched DVDs, played board games and taken the dog for walks.

Bo-o-o-RING!

No-one wanted to hear about that!

But my new teacher did.

“Now I want everyone to write about the most exciting day of your holidays,” she said. “As much as you can. But at least a page. Away you go!”

Away everyone went.

Except me.

Chapter 2
Making It Up

I SAT AND LOOKED at my blank page. I closed my writing book. Soon my teacher came over.

"What did you do over the holidays, Joel?" she asked.

"Nothing," I said.

"Nothing? Absolutely *nothing*?" said my teacher.

"Well, nothing that I can write about," I said.

"You must have done *something*," my teacher said.

"But I didn't!" I said. "I had a really, really boring holiday!"

My new teacher looked at me. Now she looked as if she felt a bit sorry for me.

"Well, if you really didn't do anything exciting," she said, "then make something up!" And she winked at me. And something sort of ... **sparkled**... in the air around her.

I watched her walk away.

Make it up, she'd said. Make it up…

All right then, I thought, *I will. I'll make it up. And I'll really make it exciting!*

I thought about all the things I'd done with Natalie and Gran. The park. The library. The pool. An ice-cream at the shops. A pizza. Not at all exciting! But maybe it could be… I picked up my pen and wrote:

We went to the library for story time.

That was true. But then I started to imagine.

You wouldn't believe it. It was my favourite author, Anastasia Olivetti. She was making a surprise visit to our local library!

I told Anastasia Olivetti I was a big fan of hers, but that I was just a little disappointed with the ending of her last book.

"So how would you have ended it?" Anastasia Olivetti asked me.

I told her. Anastasia Olivetti was so pleased with my ending, she said she'd dedicate her next book to me.

I read over what I'd written. *Pretty good*, I thought. *Great start!* I went on.

I wrote about going to the ice-cream shop. Mr Gelati makes the best ice-cream.

But today Mr Gelati was looking sad. "People are tired of all my flavours," he said. "They want something new. Something different. I can't think of anything different at all!"

I thought about it. "How about putting jelly babies in the ice-cream?" I said. "That would be different!"

"Wow!" said Mr Gelati. "That's a great idea! What an ice-cream! I'll call it 'Joel's Jelly Baby Freeze'!"

Mr Gelati

I wrote about Gran taking us to the Pizza Shack at lunchtime.

Outside the Pizza Shack, there was a band and a lot of people. They all looked as if they were waiting for something.

And they were.

When Natalie and I pushed the door open, the band started to play. All the people cheered wildly.

Natalie and I were the Pizza Shack's one millionth customers! We got free pizza for a year!

Excellent! I thought. I'd already filled two pages!

My teacher looked over my shoulder. "I knew you could do it, Joel," she said. "That's wonderful! Will you let me read it to the class?"

And she did.

"So Joel had a very, very exciting holiday, didn't he?" she finished. She winked at me again. And again, something sort of … **sparkled** … in the air around her.

My paper was still sparkling when she gave it back to me.

Chapter 3

Something Weird Happens

THEN I LOOKED AT MY PAPER SADLY. *I wish my holiday* had *been exciting*, I thought. *I wish I hadn't had to make it all up*.

"Now, for homework over the weekend," our new teacher said, "I want everyone to write about your pet. But not the pet you've really got."

She smiled. "I want you to write about the pet you'd like to have, if you could have any pet you wanted. Use your imaginations!"

I just stared at our teacher. Use your imaginations, she'd said. I felt as if I'd used up all my imagination already!

I'd imagined meeting a famous author and giving her a great idea.

I'd imagined inventing a great new ice-cream flavour.

I'd imagined winning free pizza for a year. I had no imagination left!

So I didn't even look at my homework on Friday night. *I'll think about it later*, I thought.

On Saturday, Natalie, Mum and I went to the library and the shops.

"Maybe we'll get a pizza as well," said Mum.

We went to the library first. There was a crowd of people inside.

"What's going on?" I asked.

"There's a famous author visiting," a girl said.

"An author?" I said. "Who?"

"Anastasia Olivetti!" the girl said.

Library

Anastasia Olivetti! I couldn't believe it.

I'd made up a story about Anastasia Olivetti visiting our library—and now here she was!

My very favourite author was right here in our library! I just had to say hello to her.

I went over to the little table where Anastasia Olivetti was signing books. I waited to speak to her. And then something weird happened.

Anastasia Olivetti looked up and saw me. And she…well, she seemed to know me!

She jumped to her feet. “Joel!” she said. “My friend Joel!” She gave me a big hug. “I’ve used that ending you told me about,” she said. “It’s so good! My book’s all finished! I dedicated it to you. Thank you, thank you!”

This was weird. Weird! It was as if what I’d made up had actually happened. I couldn’t get out of the library fast enough.

Chapter 4

More Weird Things Happen

THEN SOMETHING ELSE weird happened. Natalie and I walked towards Mr Gelati's ice-cream shop. We could see his shop was full. In fact, it was more than full. There were people crowded inside, and people out the front of the shop.

"Looks like Mr Gelati's got lots of customers!" said Natalie.

Mr Gelati was serving ice-cream as fast as he could, but then he looked up and saw us. He stopped serving.

"Wait!" he said to everyone. "Stop! Look! It's Joel—the inventor of Joel's Jelly Baby Freeze!"

Mr Gelati called to me, "Joel! Wait!" He rushed out with two huge ice-creams in his hands. "Joel's Jelly Baby Freeze is selling like crazy!" he said. "Everyone wants it! Thank you, thank you!"

Weird!

Mr Gelati

Then Mum came along. “Ready for pizza?” she said. “Let’s get a family-size Shack Special with double topping!”

As soon as we walked into the Pizza Shack, the manager came over to us, smiling.

“Ah, our pizza-for-a-year winners!” he said. “Welcome! What would you like today?”

“Pizza for a year?” said Mum. “Joel, did you win a competition? Why didn’t you tell me?”

“I, um, I forgot,” I said.

This was so weird!

But the pizza was great.

PIZZA

When we got home, I thought about it.

What a day! How had it all happened? I thought. I didn't know. But it had all started when I told my new teacher I had nothing to write about. And she'd told me to make something up. And then everything had come true.

I thought and thought, but I didn't know how it all happened.

"Joel!" Mum called. "Have you started your homework yet?"

Homework! I thought. We had to write about the pet we'd most like to have. Any pet at all. Would it . . . could it . . . could that possibly come true, too?

What if I wrote that I'd like to have a horse? A *horse*! I could do better than that! What about an elephant? Or a crocodile? Or even a . . . a . . . oh, WOW! Even a *dinosaur*?

I didn't know what would happen. But I was going to find out!

"I'm going to do my homework now, Mum," I called. "Right now!"

And I did. I grabbed my notebook and I wrote and wrote.

And something weird happened...